Building Your Own Kitchen Furniture

Step by Step Instructions to Constructing Stools and Cabinets

By

Hubbard Cobb

Copyright © 2011 Read Books Ltd.
This book is copyright and may not be
reproduced or copied in any way without
the express permission of the publisher in writing

British Library Cataloguing-in-Publication Data
A catalogue record for this book is available from
the British Library

Contents

	Page No.
Step-Up Ladder Stool	1
Breakfast Bar	3
Cook Book and Recipe Filing Shelves	5
Knife Rack	7
Broom Cabinet	9
Built-In Ironing Board	11
Sink Enclosure	14
Upper Corner Cabinet	17
Kitchen Corner Cabinet	19
Kitchen Wall Cabinets	21
Base Kitchen Cabinet	24

For the Kitchen

STEP-UP LADDER STOOL

You'll find many uses for this step-up ladder stool in the kitchen, pantry, and workshop.

The assembly of the legs for the ladder stool is begun by cutting the straight one to size — 21 3/4" long. To the inside of this leg, attach a 1" x 4" support at the top. Make sure that the top of this support is flush with the top of the leg and that they join at exactly 90 degrees. Now tack the other leg, which runs off at an angle, to the other end of this support and position it so that the top outside edge of this leg is exactly 9" from the rear edge of the straight leg while the bottom outside edge is 15" away from the rear edge of the straight leg. Now, laying a square along the straight leg, mark off the angle at which the bottom of the other leg must be cut to rest level. Use the same procedure for cutting off the top end of this leg. The top support should have its end cut off flush with the outside edge of the leg. Install the two additional 1" x 2" supports, and then make up the other leg assembly in the same manner. The two pairs of legs are joined in the back by two strips of 1" x 4". One of these fits flush under the top, the other flush with the bottom rung support.

Steps for the ladder can now be cut and installed. The top for the stool is cut from 1" stock 10 3/4" x 14 1/2". A 1" x 2" is nailed on the underside of the top in such a way that it can be fastened to the top support between the legs.

After the ladder has been assembled, round off all edges or bevel them with a plane or wood rasp.

Materials List

2 pieces 1" x 4" x 24"
2   "   1" x 4" x 21 3/4"
2   "   1" x 4" x 13 1/2"
2   "   1" x 4" x 12" (steps)
2   "   1" x 4" x 10"
2   "   1" x 2" x 13"
2   "   1" x 2" x 11"
2   "   1" x 2" x 9"
1   "   1" x 10 3/4" x 14 1/2" (top)

Materials Totals

1" x 4" — 13' 6 1/2"
1" x 2" — 5' 6"
(Remainder as itemized above)

Step-up Ladder Stool

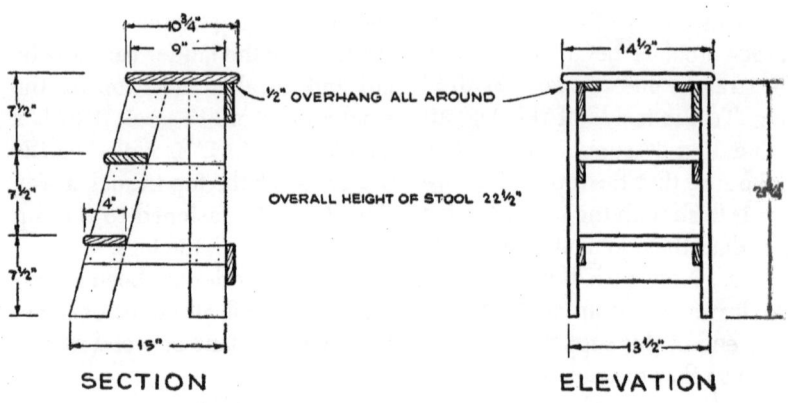

SECTION

ELEVATION

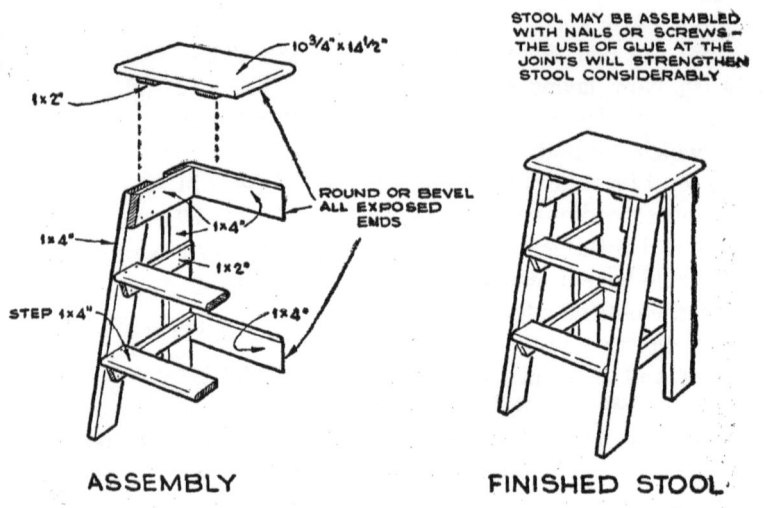

ASSEMBLY

FINISHED STOOL

BREAKFAST BAR

This breakfast bar can be attached to existing kitchen cabinets, or to the wall and base cabinet illustrated elsewhere, or directly to a wall.

The top of the bar is made up of two pieces of 3/4" plywood. These should be fastened together with screws and wood glue. The top is then fastened to the wall or cabinet with a 3" x 3 1/2" angle iron at each end. The dimensions of the bar top can be varied to meet individual requirements. The outer edge of the bar top is supported at one end by means of a 2" x 2" leg. The other end is supported by the tray storage rack and a short leg. To install the long leg, first set a strip of 2" x 3" that is 8" long on the floor, and then place the 2" x 2" leg against this and the bar top to get the proper angles for the end cuts on the leg. Cut the leg to size — 25 1/2" — and then fit a 1/2" dowel into the 2" x 3" base. The dowel should extend 2" or so above the 2" x 3" base and should run at the same angle as the leg. Drill a hole in the leg the same depth as the portion of the dowel above the base, fit the dowel into the leg, and slip the leg in under the bar top. Fasten the leg to the top by running a long screw down through the top, and then install a 3/4" angle iron.

The tray rack on the other side of the bar top is fastened to the top with two 1" x 1" wood cleats. Cut the two sides of the rack and the bottom piece and fasten in place. A 2" x 3" base should be fastened to the floor under the tray, and a strip of 2" x 2" that is 10 1/2" long run between this and the bottom of the tray storage rack. Angles of short and long legs must be equal.

The bar top can be covered with linoleum or stainless steel with steel or aluminum edging. The seam where the back of the bar joins the wall can be covered with a strip of 1/2" quarter round.

Materials List

2 pieces 2" x 3" x 8 1/2"
1   "   2" x 2" x 25 1/2"
1   "   2" x 2" x 7 1/2"
2   "   1" x 1" x 12"
2   "   3/4" plywood 13" x 56"
1   "   1/2" plywood 13" x 28 1/2"
1   "   1/2" plywood 13" x 18"
1   "   1/2" plywood 10" x 3"
2   "   angle irons 3" x 3 1/2"
1 angle iron 3/4"

Materials Totals

2" x 3" — 1' 5"
2" x 2" — 2' 9"
1" x 1" — 2'
3/4" plywood 56" x 26"
(Remainder as itemized above)

Breakfast Bar

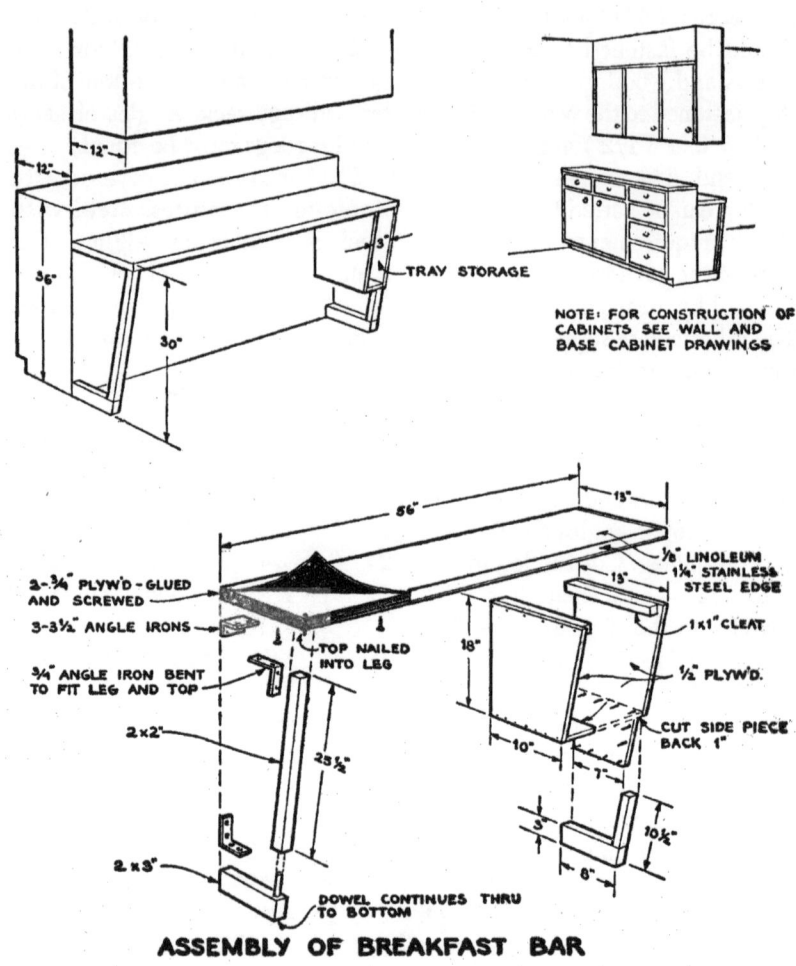

ASSEMBLY OF BREAKFAST BAR

COOK BOOK AND RECIPE FILING SHELVES

These cook book and recipe filing shelves make an excellent addition to your kitchen cabinets.

Cut the two side pieces to size, and then cut a rabbett along the top and bottom inside edge 1/4" deep and 3/4" wide. Cut a rabbett along the inside of the back edge 1/4" deep and 1/2" wide. 3 9/16" up from the bottom edge of each piece, cut a rabbett 1/4" deep and 3/4" wide. This is for the shelf directly above the two small drawers. Now cut the top and bottom piece of the cabinet to size and cut a rabbett in each on the back edge 1/4" deep and 1/2" wide. The top and bottom pieces should each measure exactly 9 1/4" wide by 13 1/4" long. Cut the center shelf to this same size, and then assemble the pieces. The back of the cabinet is made out of 1/4" plywood, and this too can now go into place. A 9" dividing strip between the two drawers should be cut out of 3/4" stock midway between the bottom of the cabinet and the shelf.

The front of each drawer is made out of 3/4" stock. 3/16" up from the bottom inside edge in this piece, cut a rabbett 1/4" deep and 1/8" wide for the bottom piece of the drawer. On the inside surface of each end of the front piece, cut a rabbett 1/2" deep and 3/8" wide for the side pieces. The sides of each drawer are made out of 3/8" stock, and each needs a rabbett 1/4" deep and 1/8" wide on the bottom inside edge 3/16" up from the bottom to accommodate the bottom of the drawer. An additional rabbett, 1/4" deep and 3/8" wide, is also required 1/4" in from the back edge for the back of the drawer. Cut the back piece and bottom piece to size and assemble. Sand down any high points or rough spots in the drawers.

Materials List

2 pieces 3/4" x 9 1/4" x 18"
2 " 3/4" x 9 1/4" x 13 1/4"
1 " 3/4" x 9" x 13 1/4"
2 " 3/4" x 5 7/8" x 3 1/2"
4 " 3/8" x 3 1/2" x 8 3/4"
2 " 3/8" x 3 5/16" x 5 1/8"
1 " 1/4" plywood
    17 1/2" x 13 3/4"
2 " 1/8" hardboard
    5 1/8" x 8 1/2"
2 wood knobs

Materials Totals

3/4" x 9 1/4" — 5' 2 1/2"
3/4" x 5 7/8" — 7"
3/8" x 3 1/2" — 2' 11"
3/8" x 3 5/16" — 10 1/4"
(Remainder as itemized above)

Cook Book and Recipe Filing Shelves

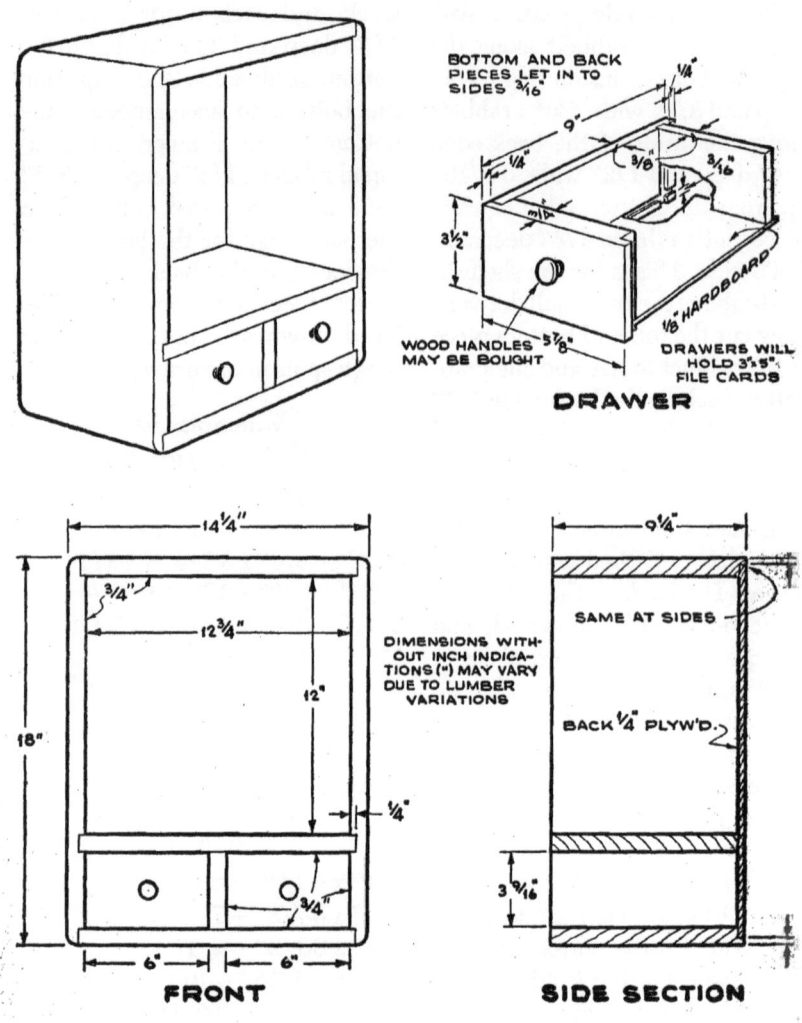

KNIFE RACK

Kitchen knives will keep their cutting edge much longer if they are placed in a knife rack rather than in a drawer with other metal objects that dull and knick the blades. This procedure is also a good safety measure, for the rack is out of a child's reach.

The top of the rack is made out of a piece of 3/4" stock. The ends can be rounded down with a plane and a wood rasp. Slots in the top for the knives are made by first drilling a series of holes with a twist drill and then squaring up the sides with a small wood chisel carefully.

The back and face of the rack are made out of 1/4" plywood. Cut them to size, leaving the top flat. After they are in place, the top can be rounded down to conform with the rounded top containing the knife slots. Tack the slotted top to the plywood back, and then install the side sections of the rack, fastening it also with tacks.

The upper section of each side piece is 5" long and extends down along the sides in a straight line. The lower sections of the sides are brought in at a slight angle so that the outside bottom dimension is 3". A tight fit where the two sections of the sides join can be made by cutting the ends of the side pieces at a slight angle. Sections of the sides are held in place by nailing them to the back of the rack. When the sides are in place, round off the top with a wood rasp to match the curvature of the top of the rack.

Holes should be drilled at the top and bottom of the back piece for nails or screws to attach the rack to the wall.

The divider strips can now be cut to size and fastened to the back plywood. After this, the front or face plywood can go on, and the top of the front and back plywood can be rounded off with a rasp. No bottom is required on the rack — it would only serve to catch dust and dirt.

Materials List

2 pieces 1/4" plywood
        6" x 12 7/8"
1   "   3/4" x 1 3/4" x 6"
2   "   1/2" x 1 3/4" x 9"
2   "   1/2" x 1 3/4" x 5 1/8"
2   "   1/2" x 1 3/4" x 4"
2   "   1/2" x 1 3/4" x 3"

Materials Totals

1/2" x 1 3/4" — 3' 6 1/4"
1/4" plywood — 12" x 12 7/8"
(Remainder as itemized above)

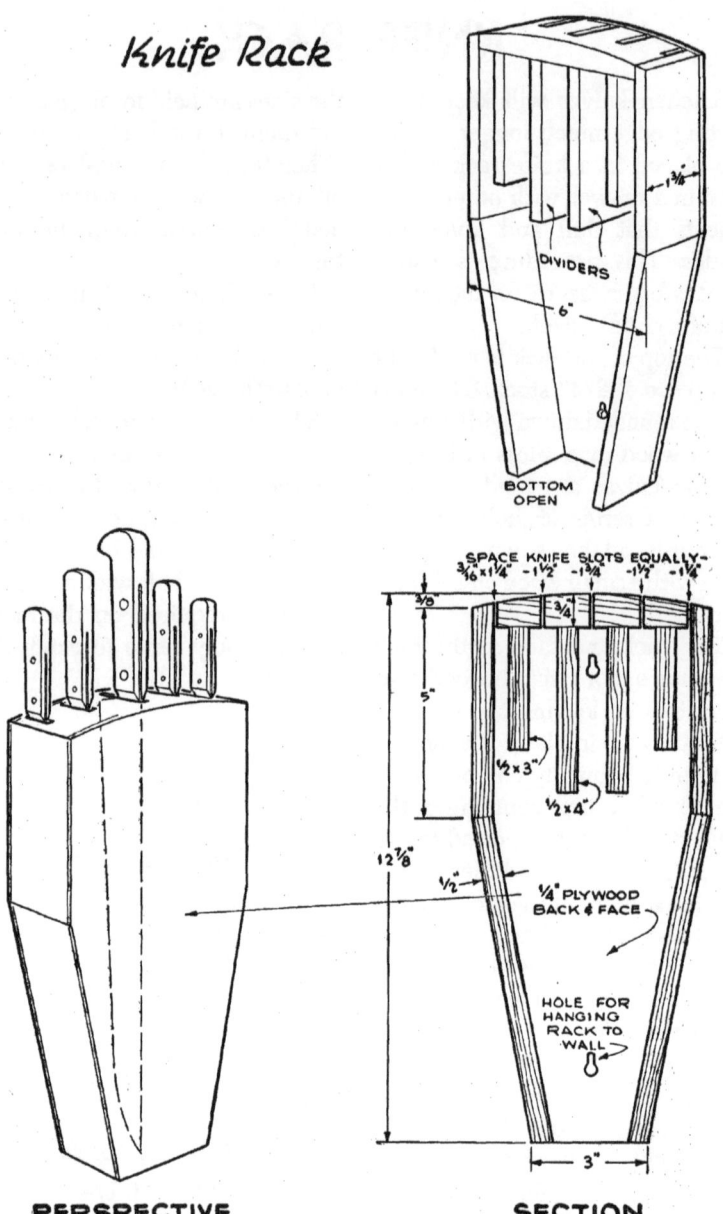

BROOM CABINET

Keeping all the house cleaning equipment in order is a good deal easier if you have a good roomy broom cabinet for storage. The cabinet shown has ample room for brooms, mops, dustpans, and other cleaning materials.

The cabinet is built up from a base made out of 1" x 2" stock. The side pieces of the base are 18" long and its ends measure 11". The bottom of the cabinet, made out of 3/4" plywood and measuring 12" x 18", is fastened to this base.

The sides of the cabinet measure 12" x 72 3/4". 10" from the top, a wood cleat 1" x 1 1/2" x 11" is attached to the inside surface to support the shelf. This cleat should be attached with wood screws. The sides and top of the cabinet can now be assembled and the back section installed. The back is made out of 1/4" plywood. Fasten the 11" x 18" shelf to the wood cleats.

A door stop is fastened along the inside edge of the lefthand side of the cabinet. It is made out of 1" x 1 1/2" stock and measures 59". It should be set 3/4" from the edge of the side, so that the door, when closed, will fit flush with the side pieces. The door itself is made from 3/4" plywood and is fastened in place with three hinges. The middle hinge is necessary to prevent the door from buckling or warping. A door latch should also be installed.

The cabinet can be left resting on the floor, but it is wise to fasten the back to the plaster wall to prevent the cabinet from being moved out of position. This can be done by using expansion bolts or rawl plugs.

Materials List

1 piece 3/4" plywood
    17 7/8" x 69 1/8"
2 " 3/4" plywood
    12" x 72 3/4"
2 " 3/4" plywood 12" x 18"
1 " 1/4" plywood
    19 1/2" x 72 3/4"
2 " 1" x 2" x 18"
2 " 1" x 2" x 11"
1 " 1" x 1 1/2" x 59"
2 " 1" x 1 1/2" x 11"
3 butt hinges
1 latch

Materials Totals

1" x 2" — 4' 10"
1" x 1 1/2" — 6' 9"
(Remainder as itemized above)

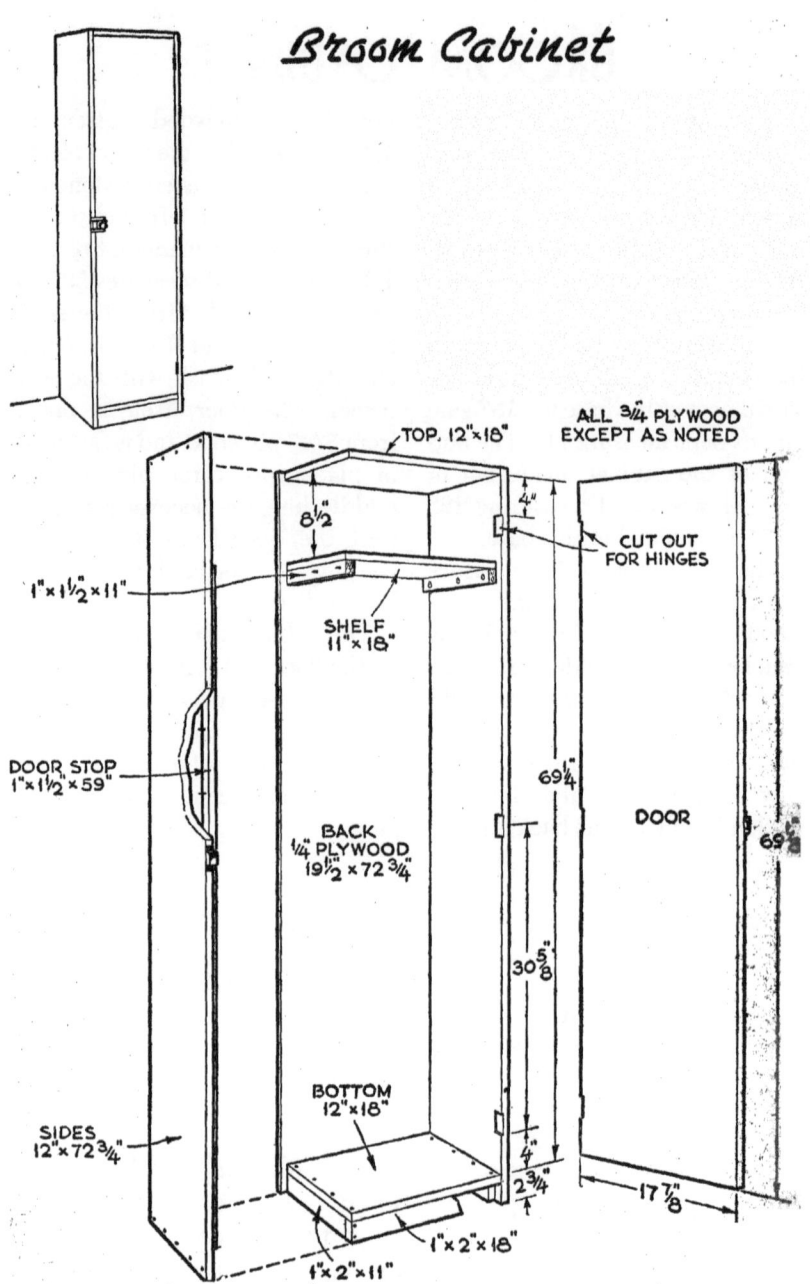

BUILT-IN IRONING BOARD

Before starting work on the cabinet, have a 20-amp duplex convenience outlet roughed into the wall in back of where the board is to be.

The sides, top, and bottom of the closet for the board are made out of 3/4" plywood. Notch out the two side pieces at the bottom outside edge for a 3" x 3" toe space. Cut a rabbett 1/4" deep and 3/4" wide above the notch and at the top of each side piece for the top and bottom pieces. Assemble these pieces and install the 1/4" plywood back. Cut and install a 3/4" strip of plywood to cover up the base of the cabinet where the sides were notched out. The cabinet can then be placed in position, a hole cut in the back for the electrical outlet, and the cabinet anchored to the wall by running screws through the back into the wall studding.

The shelves in the cabinet are supported by 1" x 1" cleats attached to the inside surface of the sides. The shelf to which the ironing board is attached has a strip of 2" x 2" fastened across the front and flush with the top of the shelf. The 2" x 2" strip should be firmly anchored in place by means of screws run in through the sides of the cabinet. The ironing board is attached to this strip with a section of piano hinge (see second illustration).

The front of the ironing board is supported by a leg made out of 1 1/8" x 4" stock 31 7/8" long. The top end of this leg should fit snugly between two 1" x 1" cleats attached to the bottom of the board and spaced 1 1/8" apart. A folding extension hinge between the board and leg permits the single leg to be pulled out from between the cleats and folded up against the board. The board is held folded upright by a strap and ring.

Materials List

2 pieces 3/4" plywood 17" x 16"
3   "   3/4" plywood
                16 1/2" x 8 3/4"
2   "   3/4" plywood 16" x 7'
1   "   3/4" plywood
                14 1/2" x 6' 9"
1   "   2" x 2" x 16 1/2"
1   "   1 1/4" x 4" x 30 3/4"
8   "   1" x 1" x 8 3/4"
2   "   1" x 1" x 4"
1   "   3/4" x 3" x 18"
1 ironing board 12" x 48"
1 piano hinge 11"
1 folding extension hinge
1 strap with ring
1 hook
3 semi-concealed door hinges
1 door latch

Materials Totals

1" x 1" — 6' 6"
(Remainder as itemized above)

Built-in Ironing Board

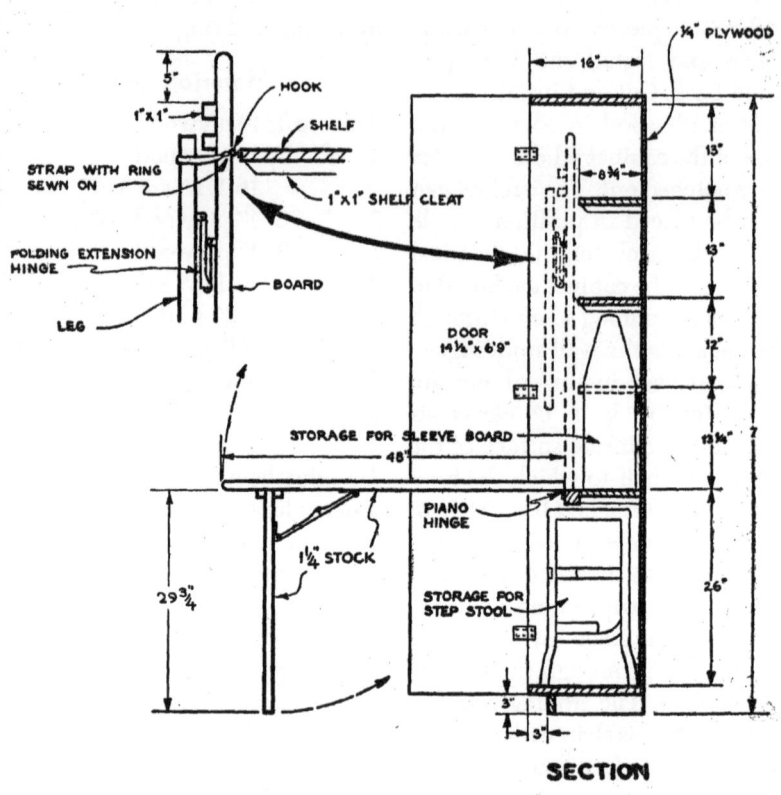

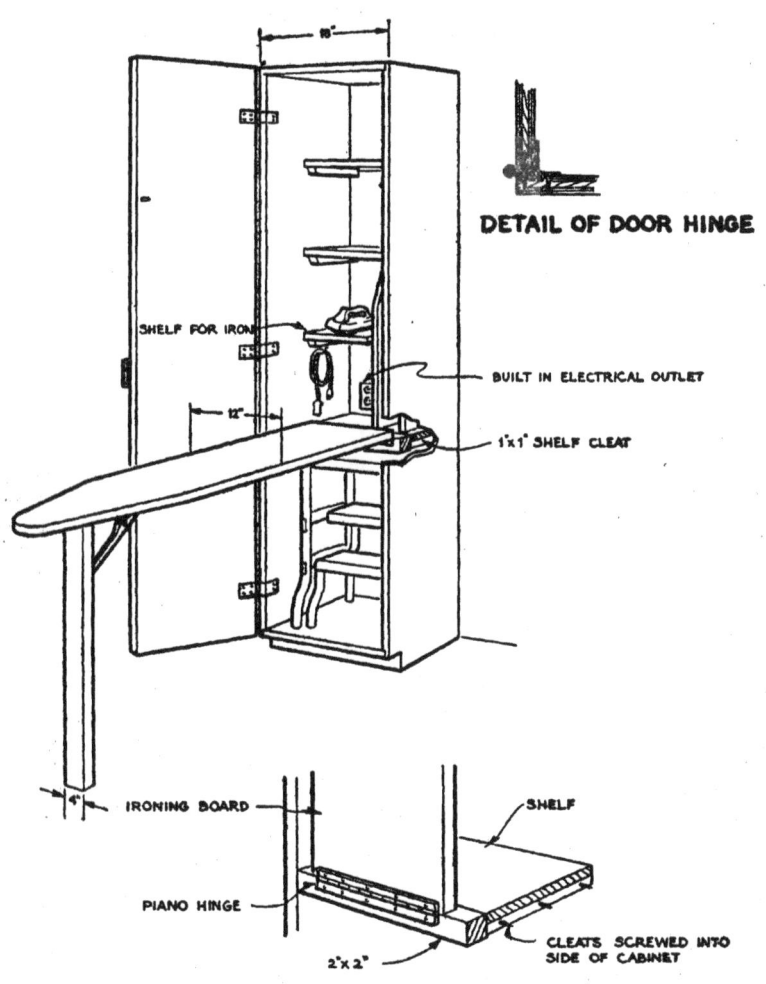

SINK ENCLOSURE

Hanging kitchen sinks can be converted into modern cabinet sinks by building an enclosure around the base.

Measure the straight surfaces on the rim of the sink. Make up the two side sections of the enclosure using the width of the straight portion of the side. To determine height, compute the distance from the edge of the sink to the floor. The rear uprights for the end sections are 2" x 2". The front uprights are 2" x 4". The bottom end of each is notched out to take a 1" x 4" board at the base. The 2" x 4" is also notched out along the bottom of the front edge to take a 1" x 3" baseboard that runs along the front of the enclosure. The top of the uprights are notched out 2" to take the 1" x 6" board at the top. End sections are held apart at the back with a strip of 1" x 10". In the center a length of 2" x 2" from the top of the back brace to the floor is fastened. The end sections are separated along the front by the 1" x 4" baseboard. This is notched out 1" x 4" at each end and fits into the notches cut on the outside face of the 2" x 4" uprights. The frame for the front section, top, and sides is made of 1" x 3" stock with a 1" x 2" across the bottom as a center divider. It should be 3" shorter than the side frames. After the frame has been made, fasten a 1" x 6" across the top in which four 1/2" x 10" vents have been cut. Fasten a second 1" x 2" across the bottom and fit two 1" x 4" at the sides and a 1" x 3" at the center. Assemble the front frame to the sides in proper relationship to the rim of the sink. Now nail the notched out 1" x 4" base piece at the bottom. Fasten a piece of 1" x 4" along the floor between the front section and the 2" x 2" piece nailed to the 1" x 10" back piece. If you want a shelf, fasten 12" x 12" metal shelf hangers to the 2" x 2" rear uprights and the 2" x 2" middle piece. The shelf can be made out of a piece of 1" x 12" or 1" x 10". The end sections and the bottom of the enclosure are 1/2" plywood. Doors are made of 1/2" plywood cut 3/4" larger than the opening. Along the edges a rabbet 3/8" wide and 1/4" deep is cut. The outside edge of the plywood is then rounded off.

Materials List

Because of the wide variation in sizes and shapes of kitchen sinks, a material list is not presented. The sink shown in the illustrations is 42" over-all.

Sink Enclosure

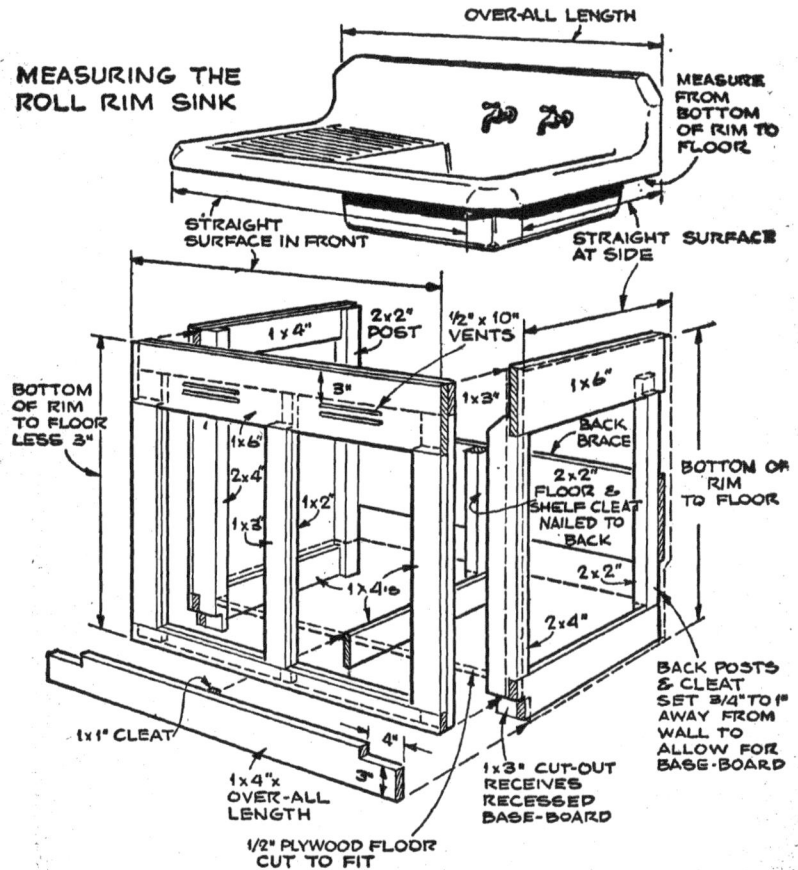

EXPLODED VIEW OF ENCLOSURE WITH RIGHT 1/2" PLYWOOD END PANEL & DOORS REMOVED.

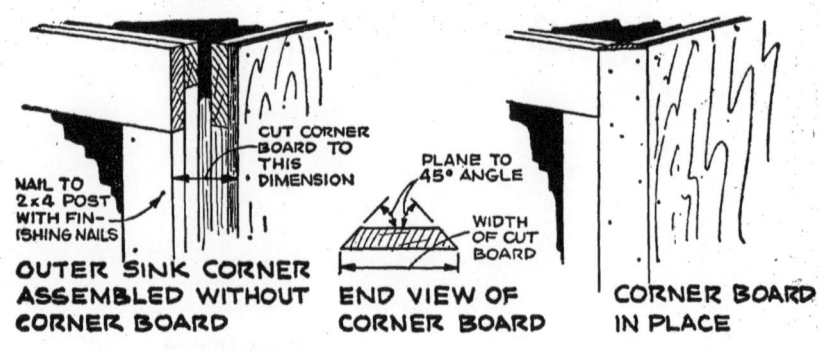

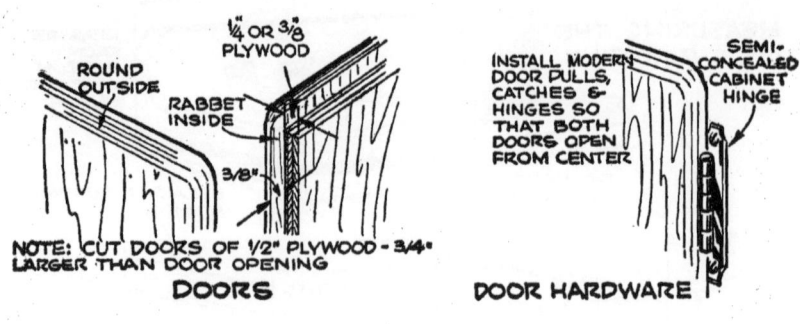

UPPER CORNER CABINET

Corners in the kitchen are often a neglected source of valuable space, which can be efficiently utilized with this upper corner cabinet.

The shelf and bottom of the cabinet are made of 3/4" plywood 23" x 23". The plan in the drawing shows how these pieces should be cut out to take the uprights. The top of the cabinet is 3/4" plywood 23 1/2" x 23 1/2". The plan in the illustration shows the dimensions of the various cuts. The uprights for the cabinet consist of five pieces of 2" x 2" stock 29 1/4" long. They fit into the notches cut out of the bottom and the shelf. The top of the cabinet fits down over them. Joints between uprights and top, shelf, and bottom are made with 1 1/2" x 1 1/2" angle irons. 24 of these are required. The two large side pieces of the cabinet are made of 1/4" plywood — one piece 23 1/4" x 30" and the other 23" x 30". The two smaller pieces are 1/4" plywood 13" x 30". The cabinet door is made out of 3/4" plywood 20 1/2" x 30". The two edges are beveled to a 45 degree angle to make a tight joint with the sides of the cabinet. There may be a difference of 1/4" in the size of the door to allow for hinges and "play" of the door. Two pieces of 1" x 2" are beveled down to a 45 degree angle and fastened to the top and bottom of one of the uprights to serve as door stops. The door is fastened to the opposite upright with cabinet hinges. 3" up from the bottom of the door on the latch side, a door pull is screwed in place. A spring catch is installed on the door and on an upright to hold the door in the closed position.

Materials List

5 pieces	2" x 2" x 29 1/4"	
2	"	1" x 2" x 2"
1	"	3/4" plywood 23 1/2" x 23 1/2"
2	"	3/4" plywood 23" x 23"
1	"	3/4" plywood 20 1/2" x 30"
1	"	1/4" plywood 23 1/4" x 30"
1	"	1/4" plywood 23" x 30"
2	"	1/4" plywood 13" x 30"

24 angle irons 1 1/2" x 1 1/2"
2 cabinet hinges
1 friction catch
1 door pull

Materials Totals

2" x 2" — 12' 2 1/4"
1" x 2" — 4"
(Remainder as itemized above)

Upper Corner Cabinet

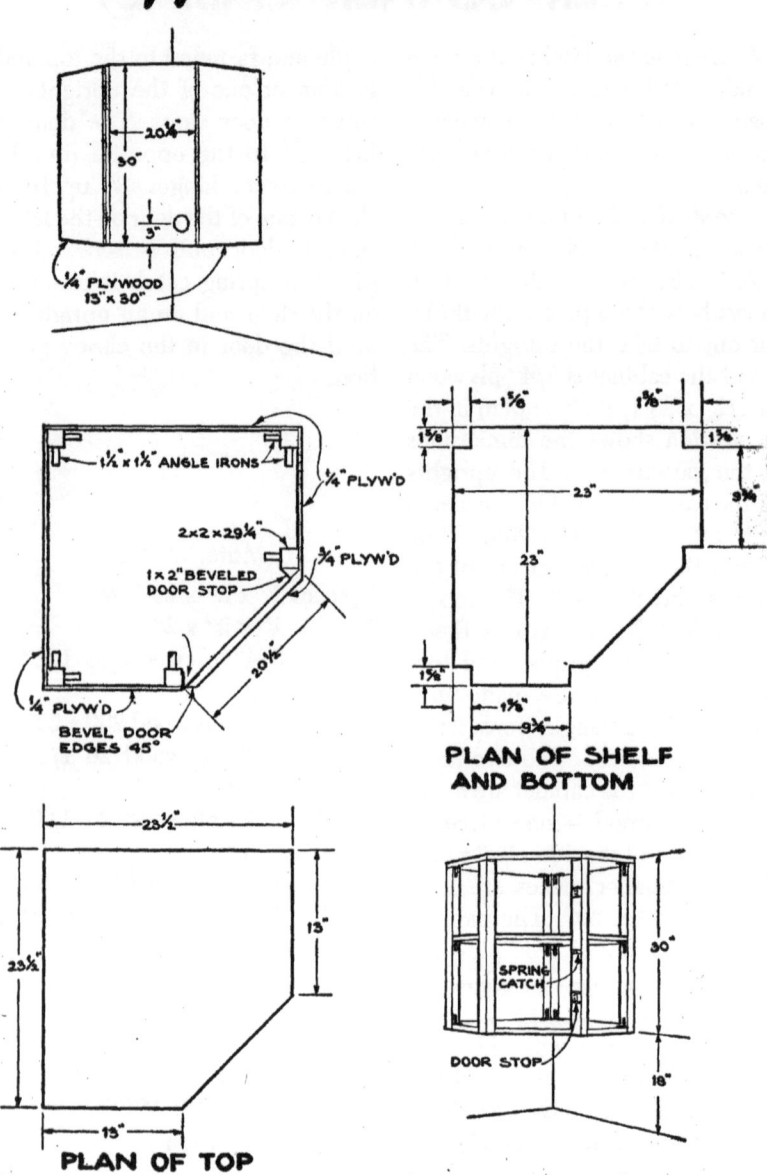

KITCHEN CORNER CABINET

Used either alone or in conjunction with base cabinets, this corner cabinet utilizes space ordinarily wasted in most kitchens.

Cut out the two shelves from 1/2" plywood 35" x 35" as indicated in the plan. These will be useful as guides for making up the framework. The three rear uprights are made 2" x 2" x 35 1/4". The two uprights in the front that serve as a frame for the door are 2" x 2" x 34 1/2". These two pieces rest on a piece of 1" x 6" notched out as shown in the detail. Uprights are fastened together with pieces of 1" x 3". The lower pieces of 1" x 3" are set 3/4" up from the ends of the rear three uprights and flush with the ends of the two front uprights that rest on the 1" x 6". A piece of 1/2" plywood 3 3/8" x 14" with the ends beveled to 45 degree angles should be installed between the front uprights at the base. Place the lower shelf in position and fasten it to the 1" x 3" strips and to the uprights. 18" from the bottom shelf, install four more pieces of 1" x 3" for the second shelf. Along the back of the cabinet, fasten two pieces of 1" x 8", one 35 1/8" and the other 35 7/8" long. These pieces should extend above the top of the uprights 6 3/4". Notch out the lower portions of the ends so that they come flush with the edges of the 2" x 2" uprights. The top of the cabinet, which is 3/4" plywood 35 1/8" x 35 1/8", is then cut to size and fastened in place.

The latch side of the cabinet is made of 3/8" plywood 24 3/8" x 35 1/4". The panel on this side should be beveled to a 45 degree angle. The hinged side of the cabinet is made of 3/8" plywood 24 1/4" x 35 1/4".

The cabinet door is made out of 3/4" plywood. The hinge side of the door is beveled to 45 degrees and the door is hinged to the upright with two 3" x 3" hinges. Two 1" x 2" beveled door stops are fastened to the upright on the latch side of the door, and a cabinet spring catch is also installed. The top of the counter is covered with linoleum in the same manner as for the base cabinet.

Materials List

3 pieces 2" x 2" x 35 1/4"
2 " 2" x 2" x 34 1/2"
1 " 1" x 8" x 35 7/8"
1 " 1" x 8" x 35 1/8"
1 " 1" x 6" x 26 3/4"
2 " 1" x 3" x 35"
2 " 1" x 3" x 34 1/4"
6 " 1" x 3" x 23 1/4"
2 " 1" x 2" x 2"
1 " 3/4" plywood 35 1/8" x 35 1/8"

Kitchen Corner Cabinet

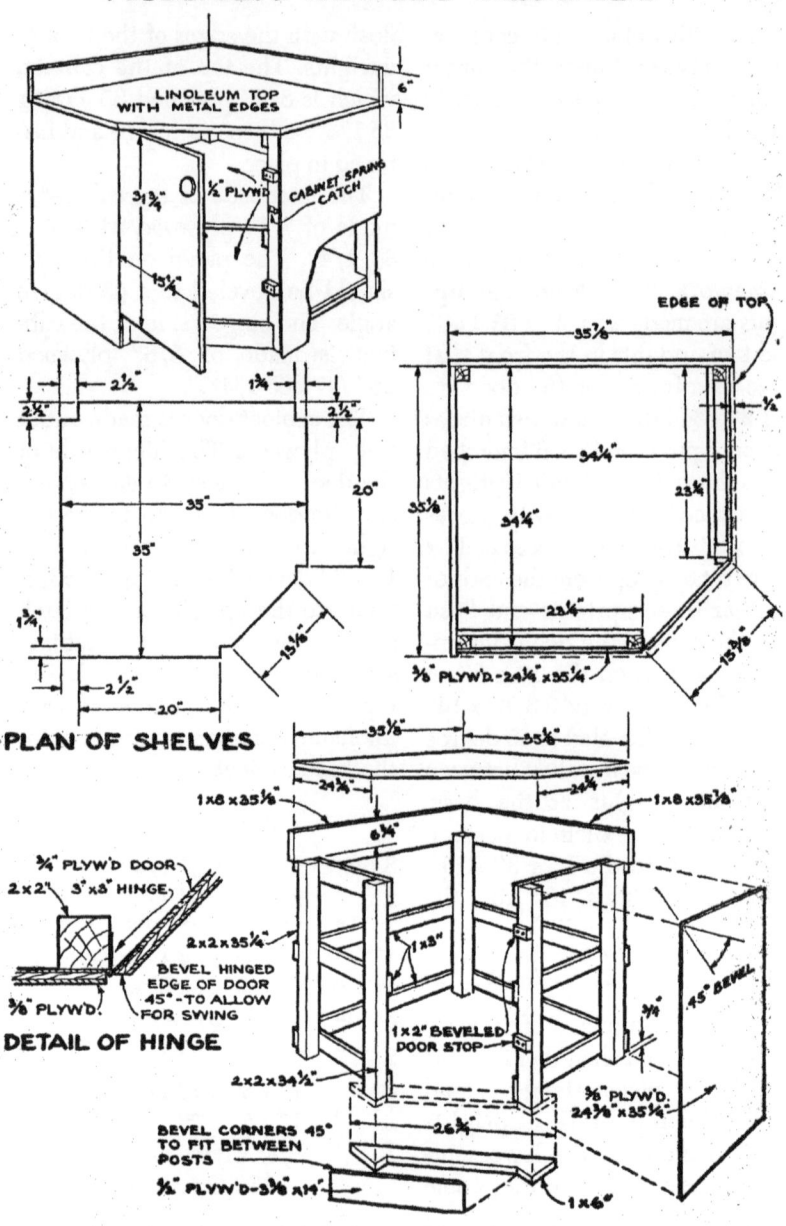

Materials List *(Cont.)*

1 piece 3/4" plywood
   15 1/4" x 31 3/4"
2 " 1/2" plywood 35" x 35"
1 " 1/2" plywood
   3 3/8" x 14"
1 " 3/8" plywood
   24 3/8" x 35 1/4"
1 " 3/8" plywood
   24 1/4" x 35 1/4"
1 " linoleum 35 1/8" x 35 1/8"

Metal counter trim 25' 1 7/8"
1 pair hinges 3" x 3"
1 door pull
1 friction latch

Materials Totals

2" x 2" — 14' 6 3/4"
1" x 8" — 5' 11"
1" x 3" — 23' 2"
1" x 2" — 4"

KITCHEN WALL CABINETS

Single Wall Cabinets

Although the cabinet shown in the drawing is 15" wide, single wall cabinets can be 12", 18", 21", or 24" wide. The sides, top, and bottom are made of 1" x 12" stock. The shelves are also of 1" x 12". The back is 1/4" plywood and the door is made of 3/4" plywood. Shelves are supported at each end by 1" x 2" cleats fastened to the sides of the cabinet.

Double Wall Cabinets

Made the same depth as the single cabinet, these double cabinets can be 24", 36", and 42" wide as well as 30" wide, like the one shown in the illustration. The same materials are used for the double cabinet as for the single ones.

For use over base cabinets, wall cabinets should be 30" high. For use over the sink, they should be 24" high. For use over the range or over the refrigerator and deep freeze, a low double cabinet 18" high is required. These cabinets can be from 24" to 42" wide.

When two or more cabinets are installed as a unit, 1" x 2" spacers are required between the units to allow the doors to swing.

Materials List

Single Cabinet

2 pieces 1" x 12" x 29 1/4"
1 " 1" x 12" x 15"
3 " 1" x 12" x 13 1/2"
4 " 1" x 2" x 11 1/2"
1 " 3/4" plywood 15" x 30"
1 " 1/4" plywood 15" x 30"
2 cabinet hinges
1 door pull
1 friction latch

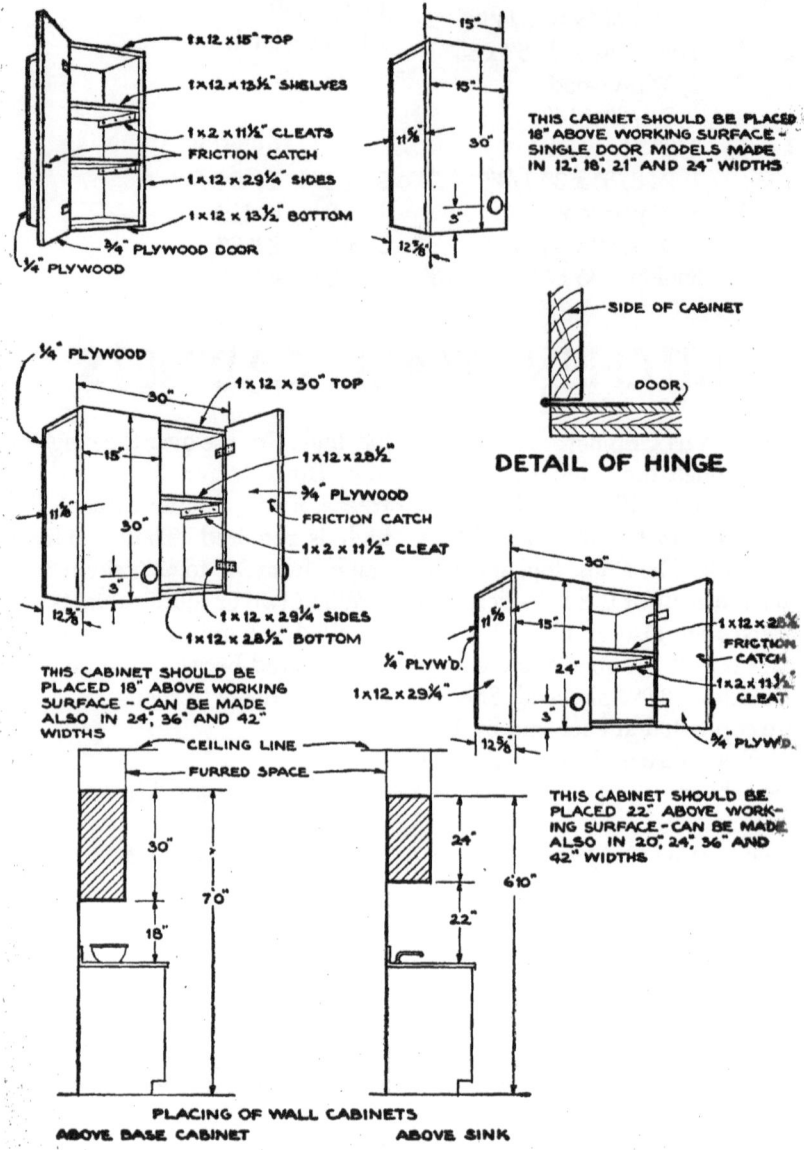

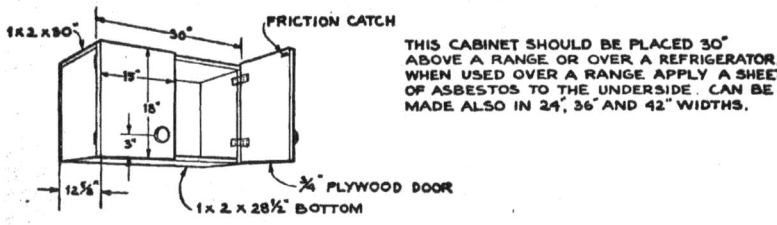

THIS CABINET SHOULD BE PLACED 30" ABOVE A RANGE OR OVER A REFRIGERATOR. WHEN USED OVER A RANGE APPLY A SHEET OF ASBESTOS TO THE UNDERSIDE. CAN BE MADE ALSO IN 24", 36" AND 42" WIDTHS.

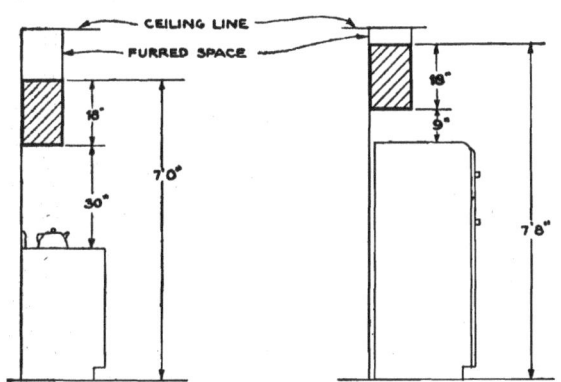

PLACING OF WALL CABINETS
ABOVE RANGE   ABOVE TWO-DOOR COMBINATION DEEP FREEZE AND REFRIGERATOR UNIT

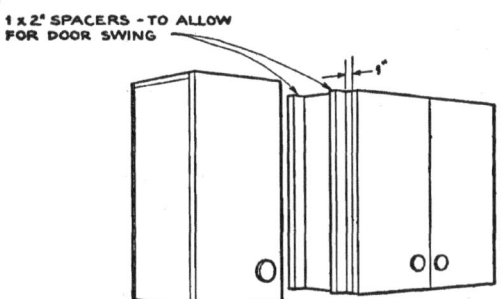

METHOD OF ASSEMBLING CABINET UNITS WITH SPACERS BETWEEN.

Double Cabinet

1 piece 1″ x 12″ x 30″
2   "   1″ x 12″ x 29 1/4″
2   "   1″ x 12″ x 28 1/2″
2   "   1″ x 2″ x 11 1/2″
2   "   3/4″ plywood 15″ x 30″
1   "   1/4″ plywood 30″ x 30″
4 cabinet hinges
2 door pulls
2 friction latches

Small Double Cabinet

1 piece 1″ x 12″ x 30″
2   "   1″ x 12″ x 28 1/2″
2   "   1″ x 12″ x 23 1/4″
2   "   1″ x 2″ x 11 1/2″
2   "   3/4″ plywood 15″ x 24″
1   "   1/4″ plywood 30″ x 24″
4 cabinet hinges
2 door pulls
2 friction catches

Materials Totals

Single Cabinet

1″ x 12″ — 9′ 6″
1″ x 2″ — 3′ 10″
(Remainder as itemized above)

Double Cabinet

1″ x 12″ — 12′ 1 1/2″
1″ x 2″ — 1′ 11″
(Remainder as itemized above)

Small Double Cabinet

1″ x 12″ — 11′ 1 1/2″
1″ x 2″ — 1′ 11″
(Remainder as itemized above)

BASE KITCHEN CABINET

The first step in making up a complete set of kitchen cabinets is the building of the base cabinet — the most useful of the entire group. This cabinet provides ample storage space as well as a linoleum-covered counter top.

The two side pieces of the cabinet are made out of 3/4″ plywood 24″ x 35 1/4″. The lower outside corner of each is notched out 3″ wide and 2 3/4″ deep to take the base strip. The base strip is made from 1/2″ plywood or 1/2″ stock and is 3″ wide and 48″ long. Two glue blocks are fastened to the back of this piece flush with the top. The bottom of the cabinet is 3/4″ plywood 46 1/2″ x 24″. The back of the cabinet is made of 1/4″ plywood 48″ x 35 1/4″. Assemble these pieces.

29 7/8″ in from the inside surface of the lefthand side, install a 1″ x 3″ stile 31 1/2″ long. In back of this piece and 29 7/8″ in from

Base Kitchen Cabinet

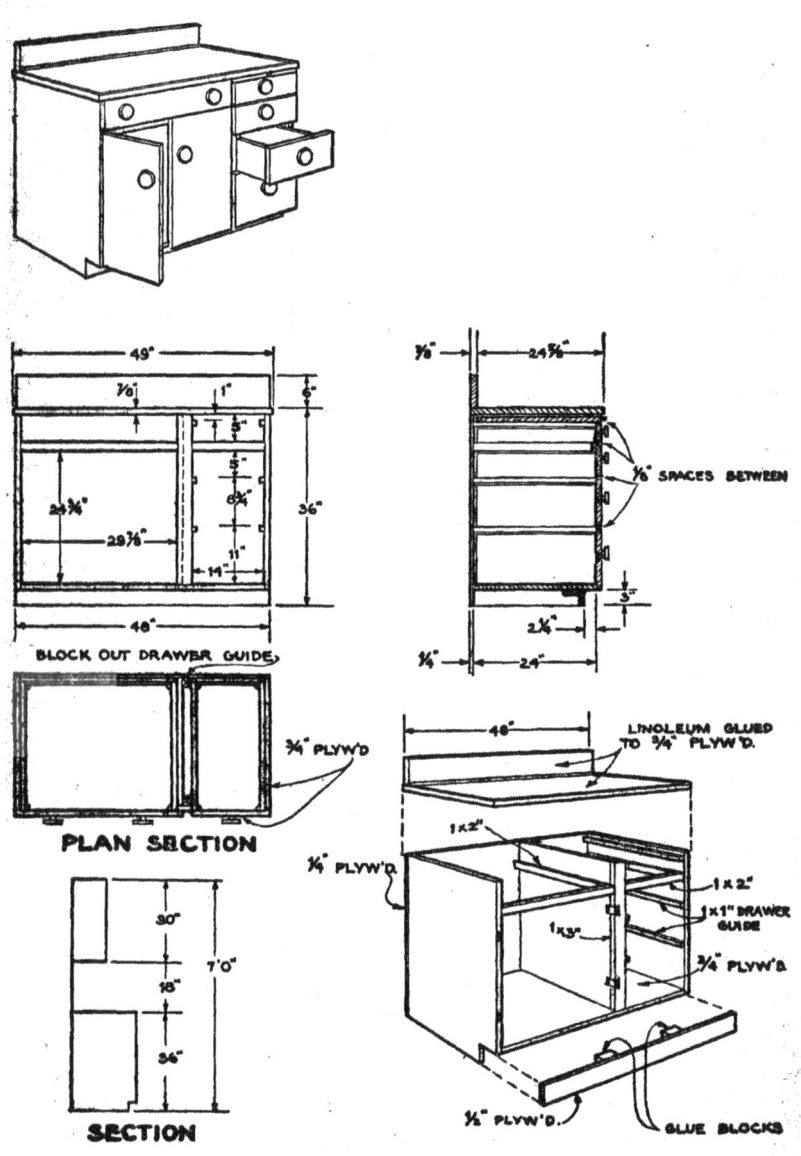

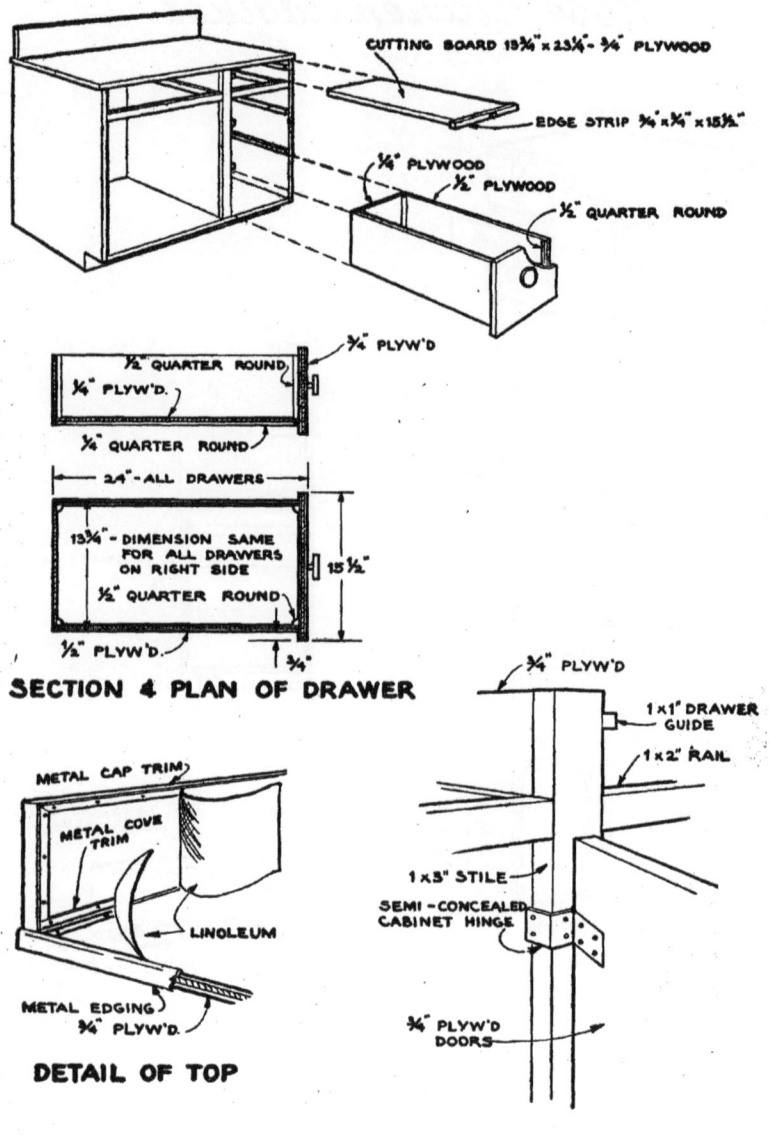

the side, install a 3/4" plywood partition. This piece should be 31 1/2" high and 23 1/4" wide. 5" down from the top of the sides, install a piece of 1" x 2" between the sides and the stile. The righthand piece of 1" x 2" should be 14" long, the lefthand piece 29 7/8". 5" down from the top, install 1" x 2" strips along the sides and on both sides of the center partition. On the lefthand side of the partition it will be necessary to fasten thin blocks of wood so that the strips of 1" x 2" are brought out beyond the 1" x 3" stile. These blocks should run the entire height of the partition as they will be needed to fasten the drawer guides into the correct position. 1" x 1" drawer guides are now fastened into place as indicated in the drawing.

Drawers for the righthand side should have an over-all length of 24". The over-all width is 13 3/4" and the width of the front pieces is 15 1/2". The sides of the drawers are made of 1/2" plywood or 1/2" stock, the back of 1/4" plywood, and the fronts of 3/4" plywood. Corners are made with strips of 1/2" quarter round, and strips of 1/4" quarter round are fastened on the bottom. However, the drawers vary in depth. The upper righthand drawer side is 2 3/4" and its front is 3 7/8". The second drawer side is 4 1/2" and its front is 6 1/2". The third drawer side is 7 1/2" and its front is 8 5/8". The bottom drawer is shown in section and plan. The side should be 9 3/4" and the front 11 5/8". The upper lefthand drawer has the same length as the others but the over-all width is 29 5/8"; the drawer side is 4 1/2" in depth and its front 5 7/8".

Materials List

1 piece		3/4" plywood 46 1/2" x 24"
1	"	3/4" plywood 31 1/2" x 23 1/4"
2	"	3/4" plywood 27" x 15 5/8"
1	"	3/4" plywood 25 1/2" x 49"
2	"	3/4" plywood 24" x 35 1/4"
1	"	3/4" plywood 13 3/4" x 23 1/4" (cutting board)
1	"	3/4" plywood 6" x 48"
1	"	1/2" plywood or 1/2" stock 3" x 48"
1	"	1/4" plywood 48" x 35 1/4"
1	"	1" x 3" x 31 1/2"
1	"	1" x 2" x 29 7/8"
4	"	1" x 2" x 23 1/4"
1	"	1" x 2" x 14"
6	"	1" x 1" x 23 1/4"
1	"	3/4" x 3/4" x 15 1/2"
2	"	1/4" quarter round 28 5/8"

Materials List *(Cont.)*

10 " 1/4" quarter round
      22 3/4"
8 " 1/4" quarter round
      12 3/4"
1 " linoleum 24 5/8" x 49"
1 " linoleum 6" x 48"
Metal linoleum counter trim 21' 5"
4 cabinet hinges
8 door pulls
2 friction catches

Upper Righthand Drawer
1 piece 3/4" plywood
      3 7/8" x 15 1/2"
2 " 1/2" plywood
      2 3/4" x 23 1/4"
1 " 1/4" plywood
      12 3/4" x 23 1/4"
1 " 1/4" plywood
      2 1/2" x 12 3/4"
4 " 1/2" quarter round 2 1/2"

Second Drawer
1 piece 3/4" plywood
      6 1/2" x 15 1/2"
2 " 1/2" plywood
      4 1/2" x 23 1/4"
1 " 1/4" plywood
      12 3/4" x 23 1/4"
1 " 1/4" plywood
      4 1/4" x 12 3/4"
4 " 1/2" quarter round 4 1/4"

Third Drawer
1 piece 3/4" plywood
      8 5/8" x 15 1/2"

2 pieces 1/2" plywood
      7 1/2" x 23 1/4"
1 " 1/4" plywood
      12 3/4" x 23 1/4"
1 " 1/4" plywood
      12 3/4" x 7 1/2"
4 " 1/2" quarter round 7 1/4"

Bottom Drawer
1 piece 3/4" plywood
      11 5/8" x 15 1/2"
2 " 1/2" plywood
      9 3/4" x 23 1/4"
1 " 1/4" plywood
      12 3/4" x 23 1/4"
1 " 1/4" plywood
      9 1/2" x 12 3/4"
4 " 1/2" quarter round 9 1/2"

Upper Lefthand Drawer
1 piece 3/4" plywood
      31 3/8" x 5 7/8"
2 " 1/2" plywood
      4 1/2" x 23 1/4"
1 " 1/4" plywood
      28 5/8" x 23 1/4"
1 " 1/4" plywood
      4 1/4" x 28 5/8"
4 " 1/2" quarter round 4 1/4"

Materials Totals
1" x 2" — 11' 4 7/8"
1" x 1" — 11' 7 1/2"
1/2" quarter round — 9' 3"
1/4" quarter round — 32' 2 3/4"
(Remainder as itemized above)

Milton Keynes UK
Ingram Content Group UK Ltd.
UKHW012217281123
433441UK00001B/65